THE JOY OF BIRTH

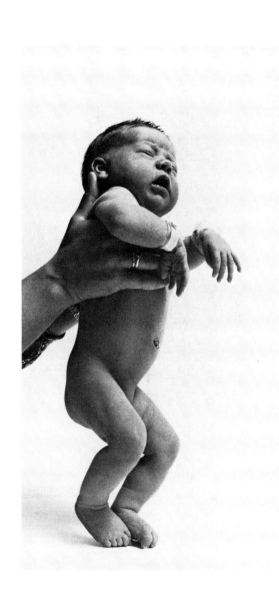

THE JOY OF BIRTH

text and photographs by
Camilla Jessel

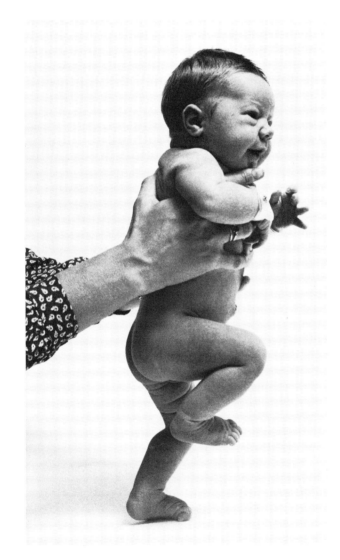

METHUEN · LONDON

For Roxi and Jeremy

Acknowledgements

The author wants to thank everyone who helped to make this book possible, especially the parents and children who allowed themselves to be photographed as well as all those who joined in the discussions about the contents of the book.

  She also thanks all the midwifery and obstetric staff of the West Middlesex Hospital, Isleworth, and the Hounslow Community Midwives; Miss K. Shaw, Miss A. Renton, the Royal College of Surgeons of England, the National Childbirth Trust, Dr. Kenneth Backhouse, Dr. James Hemming, Dr. Charles Rycroft, Sheila Kitzinger, Betty Parsons, Jenny Pearson, Sue Dale Tunnicliffe, Ralph Hutchings, Kathy MacDonald, Margaret Walker and Ti Green.

Author's note
In writing this book, the difficult question arose as to whether the embryo and fetus should be SHE or HE.
With profoundest apologies to all unborn females I finally chose HE in order to clarify in the text whether I was referring to the mother or her future baby.

First published in Great Britain in 1982 by Methuen Children's Books Ltd.,
11 New Fetter Lane, London EC4P 4EE.
Text and photographs copyright © 1982 by Camilla Jessel
Line Drawings by Geoffrey Beitz © 1982 by Methuen Children's Books Ltd.
Designed by Robert Updegraff
Printed in Great Britain by BAS Printers Limited
Over Wallop, Hampshire.

British Library Cataloguing in Publication Data

Jessel, Camilla
  The joy of birth.
  1. Pregnancy – Juvenile literature
  2. Childbirth – Juvenile literature
  I. Title
  612'.63   RG525

  ISBN 0-416-899700-6

Contents

Introduction

This is the book which I wanted for my own children, but which I could not find anywhere. I needed a text which would give direct, unembarrassed answers to their questions, but which also would convey something deeper than just the straight, biological facts of life. I wanted them to share the excitement of the expectant parents as the fetus undergoes its incredible development from one minisicule cell into a complete human being; to help them overcome any fear of the unknown by witnessing, through photography, the joyous moment of the baby's birth; and to discover also through pictures the amazing individuality and character of each new baby even in the first minutes of independent life; then to show how older children can relate to newborn babies in their family or neighbourhood.

The book grew out of discussions with my own children and their friends, and numerous parents and teachers too. It took further shape as I started to photograph, and realised that the contents should be directly based on the real feelings and experiences of the people in the pictures.

The text is written with children in mind. The photographs are for all age-groups, including teenagers, expectant mothers, future fathers, nurses, teachers, librarians, grandparents – anyone who cares about babies. Parents may wish to show the photographs to younger children too, especially if a baby is expected in the family. I would like to think of this book being shared by all the family.

Camilla Jessel.

The Unborn Baby

A new baby growing inside a mother's *womb*.
What is this baby like? What does he know and feel?

The baby is so small he could still fit into a teacup, yet already it is possible to hear his heart pounding away . . .

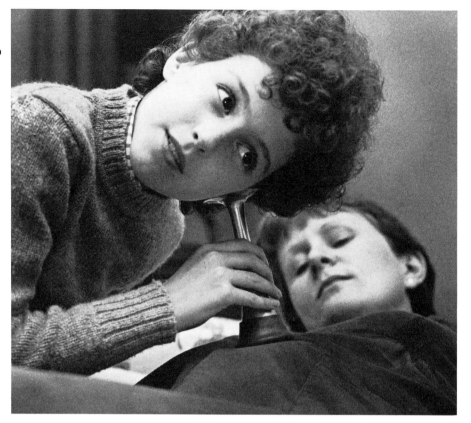

. . . and to feel the tremor of his heels as he takes his daily exercise.

'How did he get there? How did he begin?

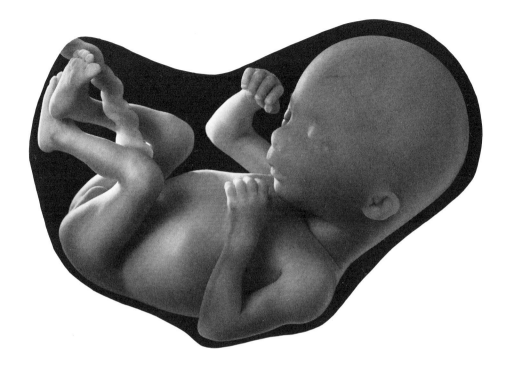

The baby grew from a fertilised egg inside his mother, an egg smaller than the dot at the end of this sentence. Every girl is born with a store of these tiny unfertilised eggs which stay inside her throughout her childhood. After she has *matured*, usually between the ages of twelve and sixteen, her eggs are ready to develop into babies. However, this can only happen if one of them has first been fertilised by a man's sperm.

Babies grow from their parents' love. A husband and wife express their love for each other by the closest-possible, most loving embrace, so that the man's *penis* enters the woman's opening, her *vagina*.

Some minute *sperms* – small cells with tails which help them swim – flow from the father into the mother. The strongest one may manage to swim its way up into the womb and join with one of the mother's eggs. The sperm is so small it is invisible except under a microscope. As soon as the sperm and the egg combine inside the mother, the baby begins to grow.

It will take almost nine calendar months – about 38 weeks – for this tiny dot to develop into a baby large and strong enough to survive outside the warmth and comfort of the mother's womb.

It takes him five weeks from fertilisation to even begin to look like a baby. At first he is a single *cell*, then he divides into two cells, then four, then eight, till, at the end of his first week, he looks like a whole ball of tiny cells:

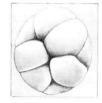

Each of these cells keeps on dividing. Some change from the basic shape and start to develop into the different parts of the baby. Some of them eventually form his hands and feet, some of them make his brain, some his eyes, some his ears. After the first five weeks he is still no larger than this little 'e', but already he has the beginnings of his backbone and his brain!

five weeks

In these early stages he is known as an *embryo*. He is safely embedded in his mother's womb, floating comfortably in a protective balloon-like sac of fluid so that he cannot be squashed or damaged, and he is kept at the same temperature.

six weeks

At seven weeks, he is still no larger than a baked bean. He looks more like a tadpole than a human being, but now he has developed tiny buds which are the beginnings of his hands and feet. From his hand-buds, miniature fingers slowly start to sprout. . . At eight weeks, his eyes have formed, but as yet he has no eyelids. His fingers are almost developed, and toes are starting to sprout from his paddle-like feet.

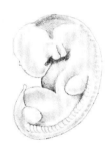

seven weeks

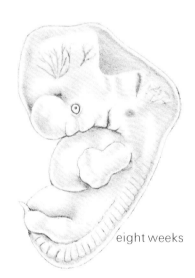

eight weeks

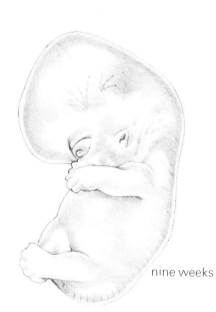

nine weeks

Hands

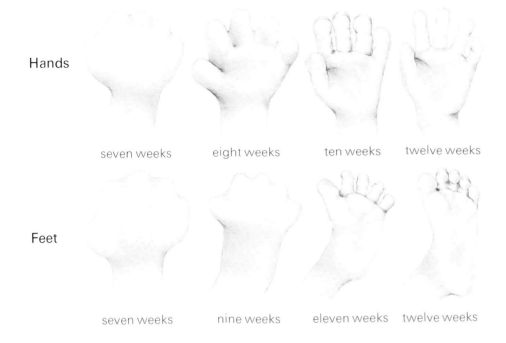

seven weeks   eight weeks   ten weeks   twelve weeks

Feet

seven weeks   nine weeks   eleven weeks   twelve weeks

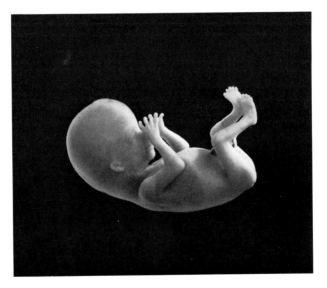

At twelve weeks, the baby is two inches long.
Thirty-two little *toothbuds* have already
formed in his jaws. He practises sucking and
breathing movements, building up strength
ready for the birth in six months' time. He now
looks unmistakably like a miniature human.
From this stage until he is born, he is known as
a *fetus*.

By the time that the fetus is four months' grown, though still tiny, he looks almost complete. He even has perfectly formed finger nails.

Hunger is no problem for a fetus: all food comes from the mother, through the umbilical cord, and is fed into his bloodstream.

His oxygen also reaches him in the same way. He will not need to breathe through his mouth or nose until he is born.

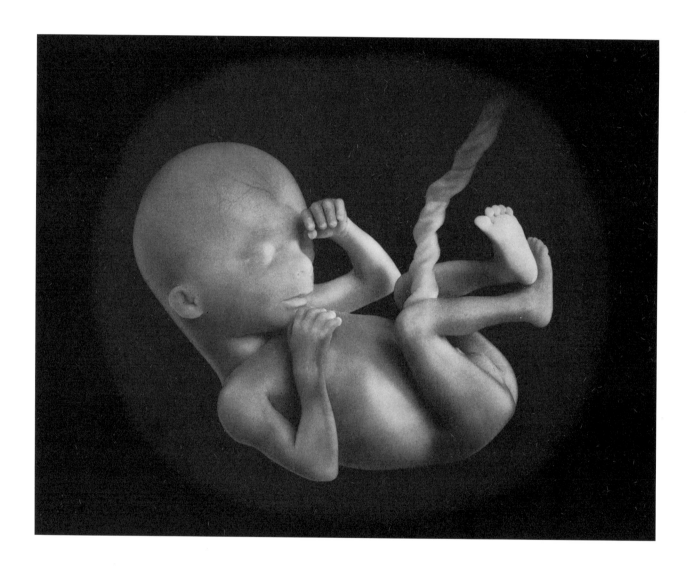

He lies there, peacefully floating, rocked by his mother's breathing, calmed by the throbbing rhythm of her heartbeat.

His brain is developing even faster than his body, but still at this stage he probably knows no more than a sense of well-being — and an instinctive desire to grow and grow.

About this stage, the mother begins to feel her baby moving inside her. At first it's hardly noticeable. It is like a finger-tip drawn very softly over the skin, a sort of ripple.

In another few weeks, the kicks are so strong, they can easily be felt, sometimes even seen.

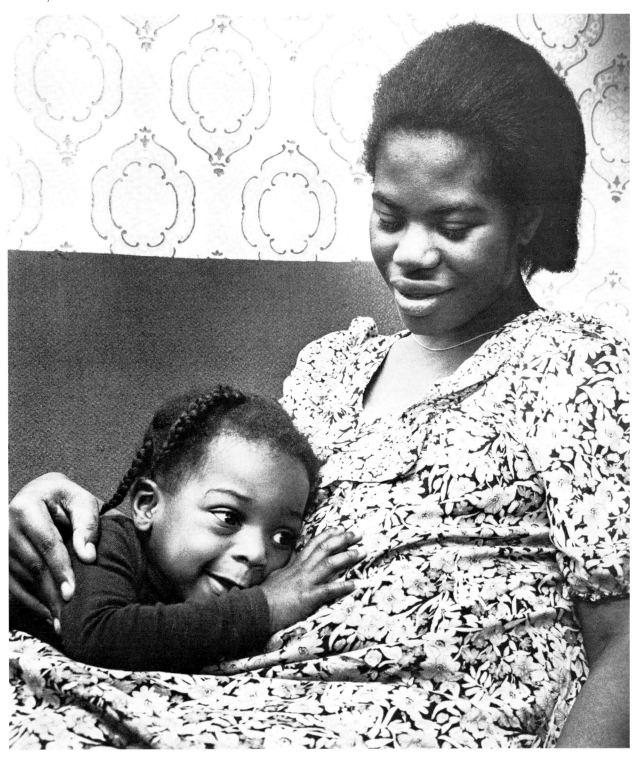

An expectant mother has to take great care to eat a healthy diet, particularly plenty of fresh fruit and vegetables. A little of everything she eats and drinks is passed on to the baby through her bloodstream. She can seriously harm her baby if she smokes heavily or drinks much alcohol during pregnancy.

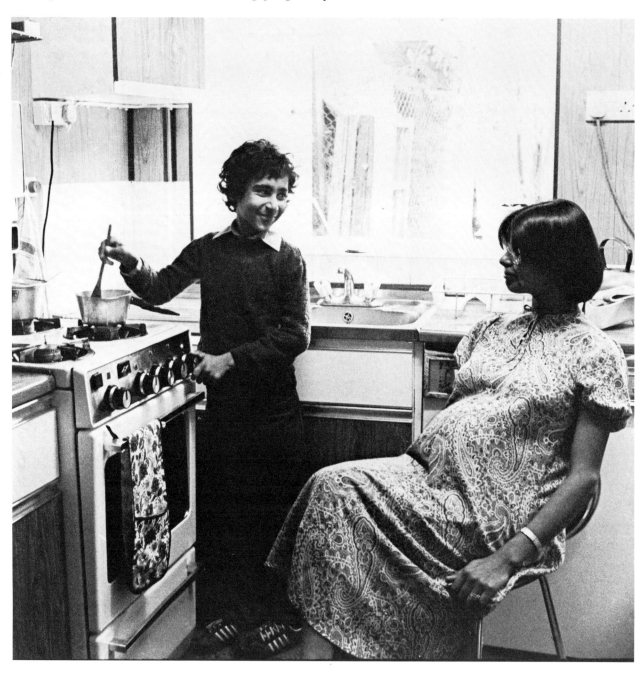

But, while she really must eat well, sometimes she feels rather sick due to changes taking place in her body. She may feel that she cannot face cooking. Then she will be grateful for help from a young friend or relative.

Later on it is difficult for her to bend in the middle so she needs help fastening her shoes, or scrubbing the bath. It is not good for her to carry heavy weights, so she needs help with her shopping . . .

. . . and with her toddler who is always tearing off and getting into dangerous mischief as soon as she tries to rest.

People can never resist trying to guess whether the baby will be a boy or a girl. In the past, a woman who only had daughters was often blamed by her husband.

Scientists have now shown that it is the man's *sperm* which determines whether the baby is a boy or girl. The sex of the baby is fixed at the very moment of *conception*, when the sperm joins with the egg.

Doctors can find out the sex of the baby before birth, but the test may cause other problems, so it is only used if medically necessary. Most people are left guessing. And many cannot resist trying out the 'old wives' theories, to see if they really work.

Janet tries the needle test, holding a threaded needle over sister Anna's stomach. Supposedly it will swing to and fro in a straight line for a boy, but in circles for a girl. This needle swung backwards and forwards, and indeed Anna had a boy. But it was sheer chance.

Another old wives' tale is that the boy lies at the front of the mother's stomach so that she appears much larger, whereas a mother with a baby girl carries her weight more evenly spread around her.

These two friends, their babies due the same week, proved the theory false: they both had boys.

The fetus has now been growing for thirty-seven weeks inside the mother's womb. The birth is officially due next week, but it could happen early, or it could just as easily happen one or two weeks late. Babies are almost never born the exact day that they are expected. In these last weeks the baby is almost ready to survive outside and is mainly putting on extra fat to keep him warm.

When he was smaller, he used to turn somersaults within his balloon of fluid inside the womb. Now he fills the oval shape but he still manages to exercise, flexing his limbs, instinctively practicing crawling and even walking movements.

By now he can also hear and see. Many unborn babies become excited and kick energetically when there is music in the room, though the sound reaching them through the waters of the womb must be as muffled as music heard by someone with their ears under the water in the bathtub. The fetus has also been practicing opening and shutting his eyes. When his mother is out in the sunshine, he can probably see a reddish glow, like a flashlight shining through a human hand.

The baby is now in position ready for birth. Most babies are born headfirst, though a few emerge bottom first (a breech birth), and some are so awkwardly positioned that the doctors decide on a cesarean operation, taking the baby safely out of a cut in the mother's stomach.

The cat is pregnant too— and she seems to understand that she and Jessica are in the same state.

Experts still argue about what the baby may be thinking or feeling at this time: Is he utterly content in the warm safety of the womb? Or does he now feel cramped with an instinctive desire to emerge and discover his own independent life?

However there is no doubt about the mother's feelings. By now she is usually very impatient to see her baby. What is he or she like? Boy or girl? Black hair, blond hair, or no hair at all? She feels she knows her baby and yet she doesn't. She longs to be able to have him in her arms to cuddle and to love.

Before she can hold her baby, though, she has to go through the process of giving birth. Many women are frightened of childbirth, and it's true that most women suffer some pain. But much of the pain can be caused because a woman allows herself to become tensed up. She might tighten her muscles through fear instead of relaxing and making the whole process easier, working with her body to help the baby emerge.

Nowadays an expectant mother usually attends relaxation classes and learns what to expect during the different stages of childbirth. Then she will be able to avoid any feeling of panic and will be able to enjoy the experience, which can be one of the most thrilling of her life.

It can be useful for anyone of any age to learn these pain-conquering techniques. Once mastered, they can be used at the dentist or when the doctor is giving an injection.

The person learning to relax must take deep, steady, regular breaths then find something to look at, say a mark high up on the wall. He actually breathes at this mark, almost imagining himself outside his own body, floating there, close to the mark.

The next stage is to practice with a friend. The friend pinches him gently at first while he continues to breathe at the mark on the wall. He must remember to keep his shoulders down—it ruins everything to hunch them up. If he can continue to concentrate on the mark while relaxing and breathing in this way, he may manage not to feel that he is being pinched.

The same, or similar, techniques are used to block out pain or uncomfortable sensations in childbirth.

In Labor

The moment this young couple's baby will be born is near.

Every half hour or so, for one or two minutes at a time, Valerie can feel a contraction—a twinge in her abdomen caused by her womb muscles starting to pull open the outlet, so that her baby can be born.

At last! At last she is in labor. Soon she will be holding her baby in her arms.

However there's no need to rush off to the hospital yet. Later a contraction will come every five minutes; then every three minutes; then every two. Then the baby will be ready to be born.

But Valerie has been told she needn't go to the hospital until the contractions are more frequent.

This gradual beginning of a labor, especially with a first baby, can continue for many hours. So Valerie and David go for a walk.

This is their last day as a couple on their own. Tonight or tomorrow they'll be parents.

Jane is having her second baby.

Her contractions came on far more rapidly than Valerie's. She had to rush to the hospital as soon as she knew she was in labor.

Jane's husband, Richard, dressed in a hospital gown, stays by her side all the time, encouraging her and sharing in the excitement as the contractions speed up and the baby's birth draws nearer.

"You're getting on very well now. It won't be long," says the midwife. She is the nurse who specializes in delivering babies, a particularly rewarding job, because she shares with the parents the joy of the baby's birth. Sometimes midwives assist doctors; sometimes they deliver the baby themselves.

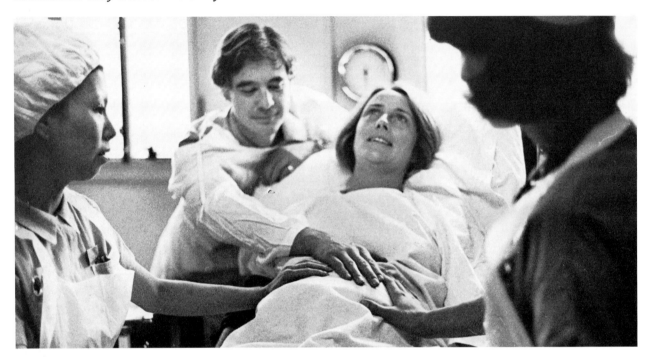

The contractions may be uncomfortable for the mother, so, if necessary, the midwife or doctor can give her an injection or a special gas to inhale to take away the pain. However if she has practiced her relaxation exercises regularly, she may not need this help.

Many mothers prefer to do without these painkillers, which may make them sleepy. They want to be wide awake to enjoy the actual arrival of the baby.

Everyone thinks about the mother's experience during birth. But what about the baby? Each time his mother's muscles tighten around him with another contraction, he probably feels something like a firm hug. This hug makes his heart beat faster, so that the blood courses more quickly through his blood vessels stimulating him and making him ready for the moment when he will have to start his independent life outside his mother.

In modern hospitals, a machine is usually set up by the mother's bed which traces the patterns of the baby's heartbeat. The midwife or doctor can then check that the baby is not becoming tired.

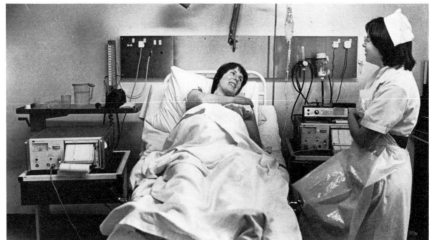

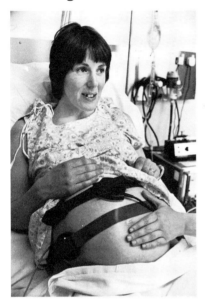

Rosina is having twins. She has a machine on each side, one for each baby. Electronic transmitters are strapped to her stomach, one leading to each machine, where heated needles trace the pattern of what is happening onto plastic paper.

The peaks on the right are Rosina's contractions, which come and go all the time.

The smaller, jagged peaks on the left show the decrease in the speed of one of the twin's heartbeats each time Rosina has a contraction.

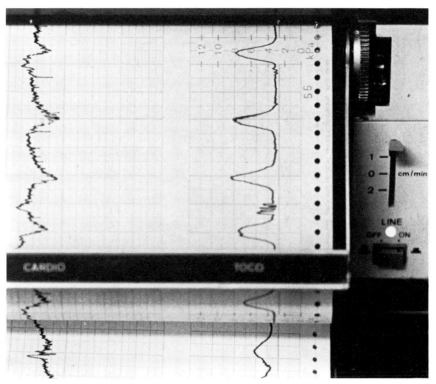

The midwife watches carefully to make sure that the peaks come exactly opposite each other. If the baby's heart does not speed up immediately after each contraction, it is a sign that he is becoming tired. Then a doctor is called, and, if necessary, he helps the baby to be born more quickly.

Both Rosina's twins are reacting well and strongly, so Rosina can relax and chat with the midwife.

The Birth

First babies usually take much longer to be born than second, third, or later ones. A first labor can last from two hours to eighteen or more. The word *labor* is used because giving birth is hard work for the mother. She is probably tired afterward, like someone who has climbed a mountain or played a hard game of tennis.

If she has a long labor, however, the first hours are usually not tiring at all. Her muscles work most strongly at the end, when it is nearly time for the baby to emerge.

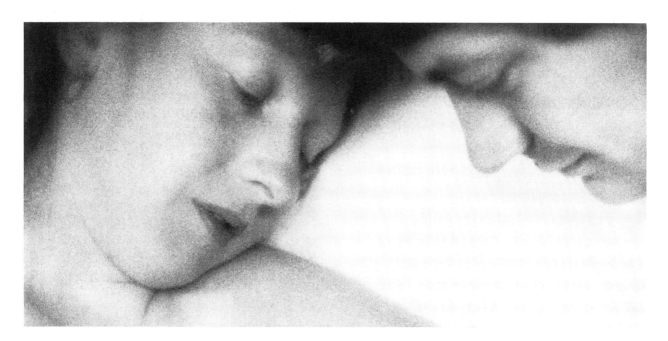

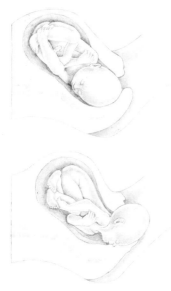

Karen is in the second stage of her labor. Her contractions have at last worked open the mouth of her womb, and now she wants to start pushing her baby down her birth canal and out into the world.

People who haven't had children often wonder how the baby manages to come out through what seems a rather narrow passage. However during pregnancy a woman's body changes. Karen's birth canal has become extremely soft and stretchy, so that it will be able to expand the necessary amount as the baby moves down.

Also to make the birth easier the baby's head is soft. The bones of the skull are not yet fully formed. The center of the head is just strong skin. So while the baby slides down the birth canal, the head becomes narrower. It returns to its normal shape after birth and in a few weeks becomes hard as the bones develop.

Karen has been pushing now for about ten minutes. She takes short rests then pushes again when she has another contraction to help her.

Excitedly the midwife tells her she can see the top of the baby's head: he or she has plenty of black hair.

So Jim, Karen's husband, gets his first glimpse of his baby before Karen. But she hasn't much longer to wait. One more deep breath and a terrific push and . . .

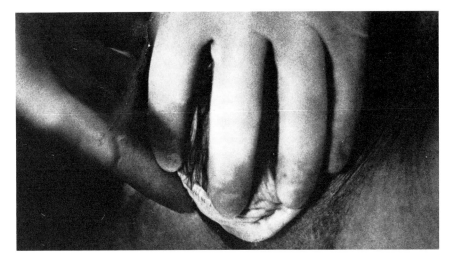

. . . the head appears, at first like a small, wrinkled bud . . .

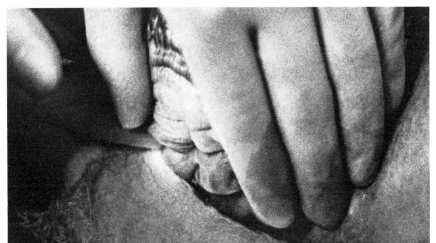

. . . unfolding . . .

. . . flowering in a few seconds into a tiny human face . . .

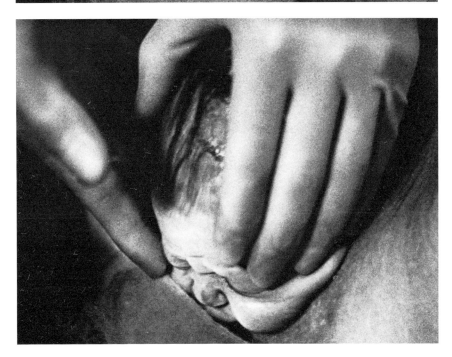

What does it feel like for the baby, the first touch of human hands gently supporting his head as he emerges?

The first rush of air on his face?

Light in his eyes used only to near darkness?

Human voices grating harshly in his ears, which till then had experienced nothing louder than muffled sounds within the womb?

First just his head appears.

Some moments later his body will follow.

The sensation of air in his nostrils, the light striking his eyes, the chatter of people's voices, everything is new and strange for the baby.

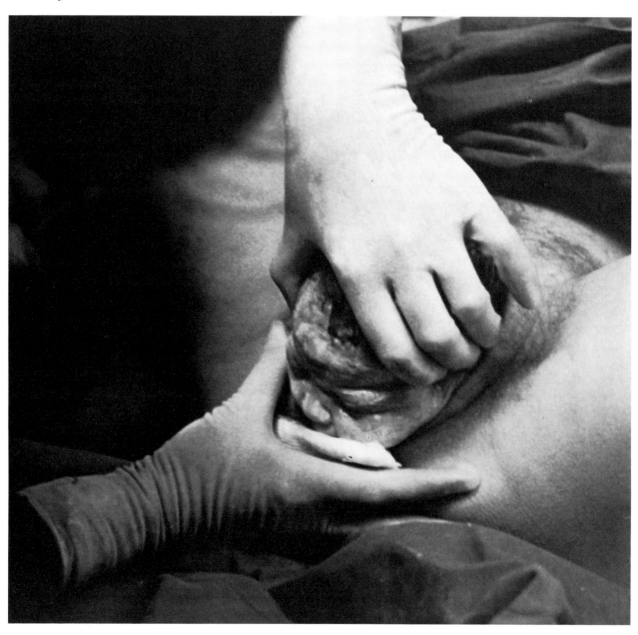

Watched and guided by the midwife, the baby turns upward, ready for the rest of his body to emerge.

One more push and he is born.

Karen reaches forward and takes her baby.

She holds him close.

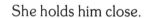
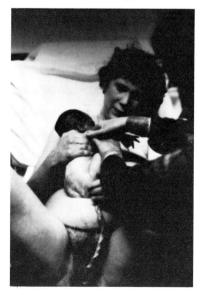

Now Karen can see her baby, can touch him, can feel him, instead of having to guess about the unseen person inside her womb.

The baby lies on her stomach, so he can still feel her breathing, the same rocking motion that he felt inside her. And he can still hear the soothing sound of her heartbeat.

Gradually he gets used to breathing for himself. Slowly he opens one eye, and then another, and wants to look around him.

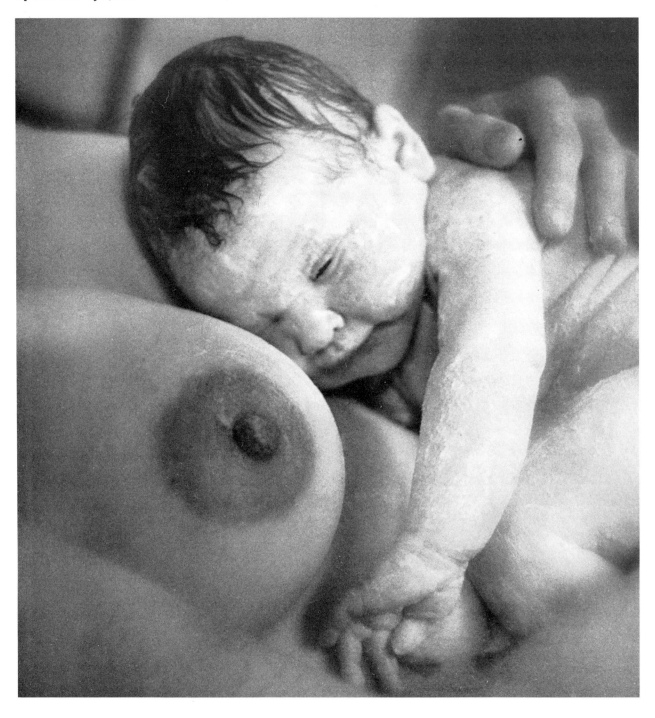

Newborns

Of course not all babies everywhere in the world are born in hospitals. Some families prefer their babies to be born at home. Then the father and the rest of the family can be more involved.

In the developed countries most babies are born in hospitals because of the extra safety of the specialized medical care.

In the hospital room next to Karen, Richard and Jane have had a boy, Adam.

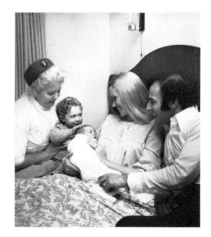

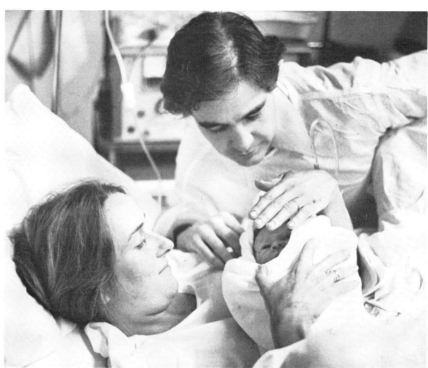

Valerie and David have a girl—they haven't thought of a name yet.

Rosina has twin girls, Polly and Joanna.

All babies are amazingly different. They may be too young to speak, but they certainly can show clearly how they are feeling by the expressions on their faces.

One new baby, Adam, is wide awake and curious about his new surroundings . . .

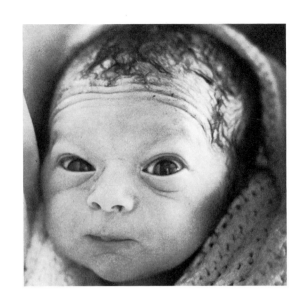

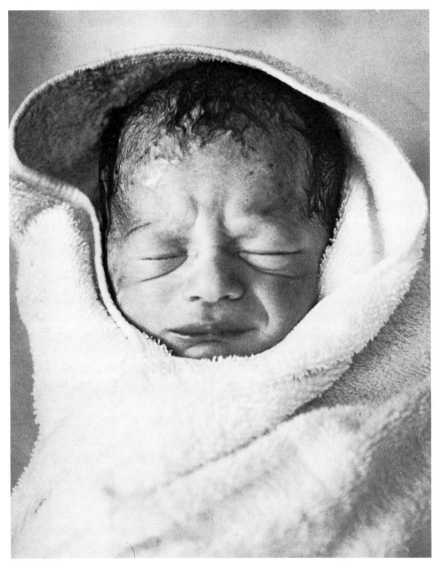

. . . while Johnny shuts his eyes and seems to be wishing he were comfortably back where he came from.

Tina not only cries—she yells! She must be uncomfortable and unhappy. Probably a good hug will put everything right.

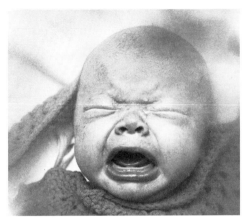

Joanna, the first of the twins, is sleepy but quite contented.

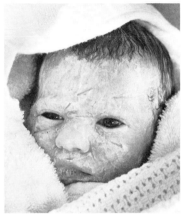

Delight in the discovery of her new life seems to shine out from the eyes of little Polly. At just nine minutes old she is clearly smiling (though medical textbooks often state that babies cannot smile before they are five or six weeks old).

Some babies, usually those born early, still have on them the white, creamy substance called vernix. All babies are covered in vernix before birth, so that their skins will not become wrinkly while they float in the fluid inside their mothers' wombs. Usually it has worn off before the time the baby is ready to be born.

Polly who, like most twins, was born early, still has this vernix on her face. Soon the doctor or midwife will wipe it away, and her skin will be beautifully soft and smooth.

Most people imagine newborn babies to be unaware of the world around them. However babies are usually full of curiosity—even excitement.

If the lights are soft, the baby may soon start looking around, fascinated by the unfamiliar sights and sounds of his new world.

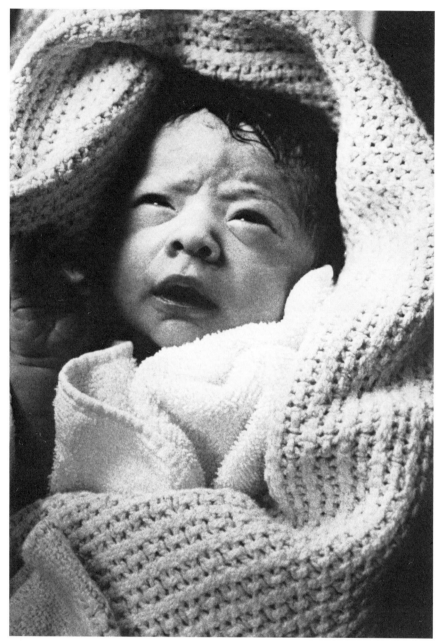

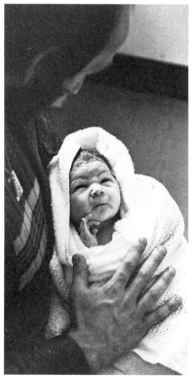

Most of what he sees is completely blurred, but if he narrows his eyes, he can focus on objects held between nine and fifteen inches from him (which is the natural distance of the mother's face when she is breast-feeding her baby).

A new baby is not yet interested in rattles or toys. But he will fix his eyes in rapt fascination on a human face: his brother, his sister, his father and mother. He seems somehow to know that this particular shape is important to him, though a face at this stage, before his sight is fully developed, cannot appear like anything more to him than a blobby pattern—eyes, nose, mouth.

The baby is enthralled. He will stare and stare—and stare.

However if the hospital lights are turned up high, they become too painfully bright for *eyes* accustomed to the darkness of the womb. The baby will then withdraw into himself and miss out on his first exciting impressions of his new world.

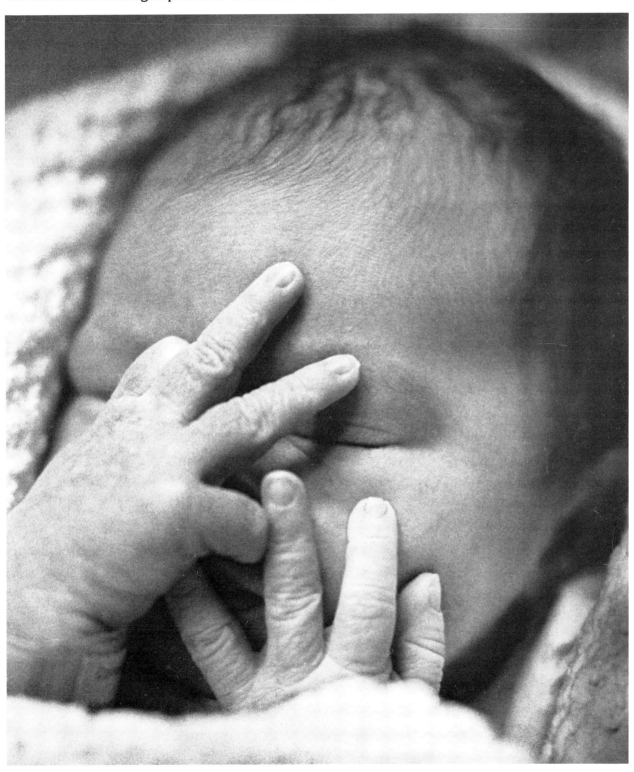

All babies have probably sucked their thumbs while still inside the womb, building up enough sucking strength in their mouth muscles to be ready to take their milk after birth.

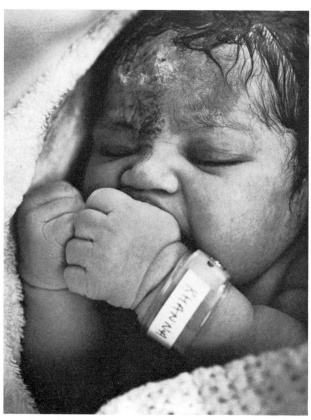

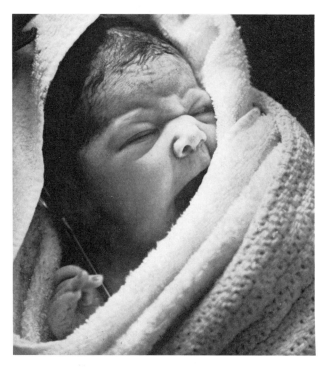

One baby manages to find his thumb right away and obtain at least temporary comfort.

Within moments of birth Jane's instinct to suck is so strong, she even tries her blanket. Anything that touches her cheek will make her turn to suck.

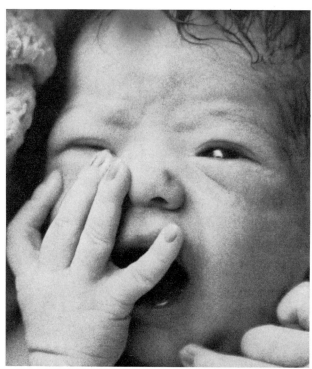

Another utters his first sad sob because, however hard he tries, he fails to trap either his finger or thumb.

As soon as possible, the baby is offered a first feed.
    Most babies are able to suck strongly for several minutes
within moments of birth.

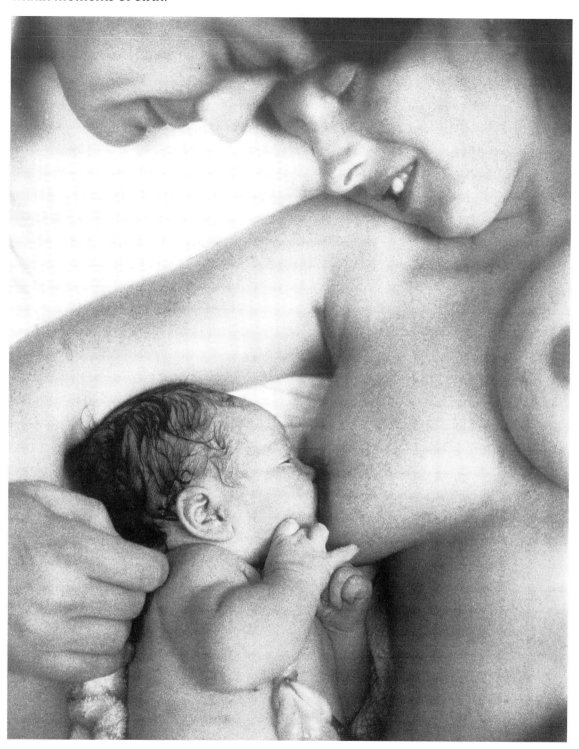

The cord which brought the baby all his food and oxygen now
lies useless, and already the baby is starting to fend for himself.

Soon the midwife takes the baby and tidies the cord, leaving a small stub which will dry up, then drop off naturally within a week or so, leaving an ordinary *navel* (belly button).

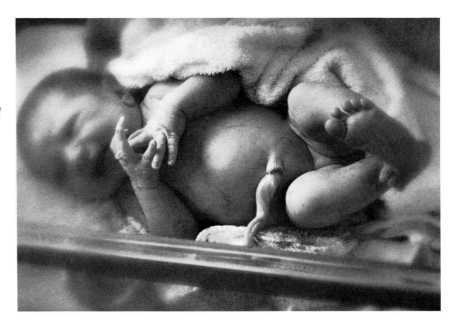

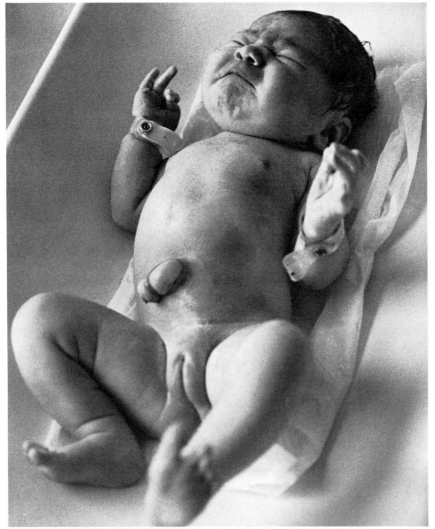

A name band is fixed to the baby's wrist and ankle so that she cannot accidentally be swapped for another baby at bathtime. (Most hospitals use two namebands in case the baby pulls the first one off.)

The baby has to be weighed. He will lose weight for a couple of days after birth, and then he should start to put it on again, but careful checks have to be made for some weeks, and compared to the weight at birth, to make sure that the baby is receiving enough food and is growing at the right speed.

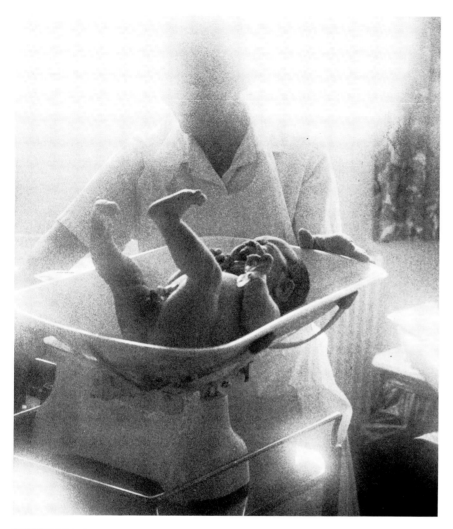

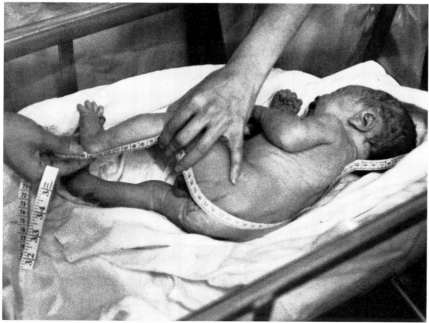

The length of the baby at birth is also important, as his rate of growth will be carefully watched and checked over the following months to make sure that he is thriving.

Then a doctor or midwife will check every detail: one, two, three, four, five fingers. . .

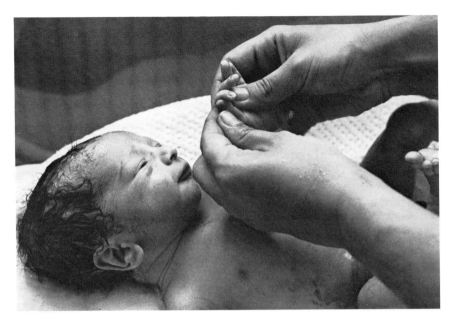

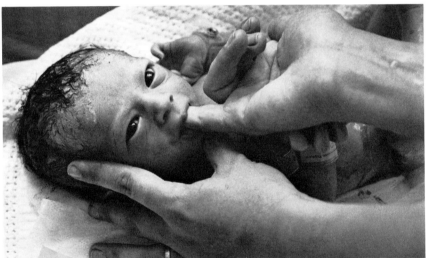

. . . the roof of his mouth: perfect. . .

. . . everything all right around his ears. . .

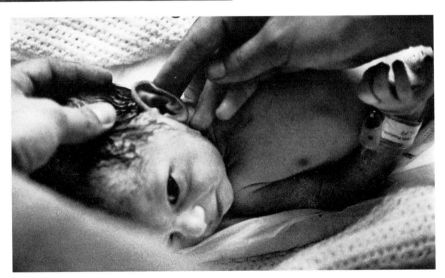

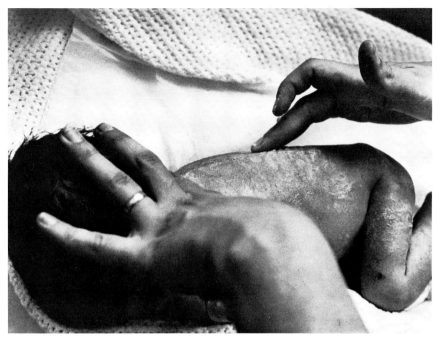

. . . every vertebra in place along the spine. . .

. . well-formed hips.

'All is well – a lovely baby!' the doctor tells the parents.

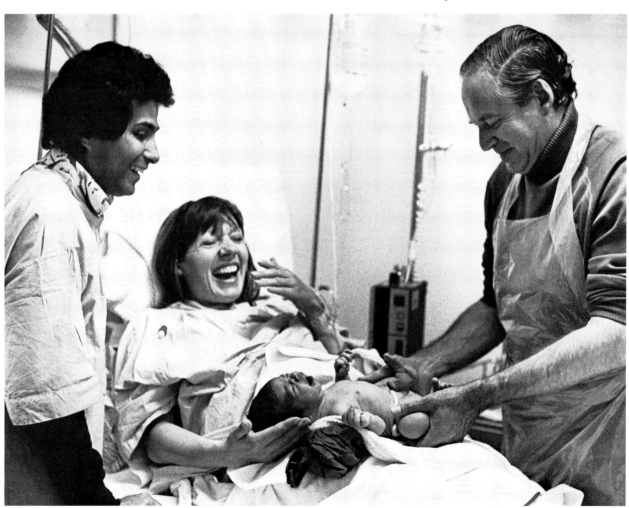

Those first exciting moments after the birth are now over.
   The baby has felt the gentleness of his mother's hands, has
experienced the warmth and sweet taste of her milk. He's
bundled up, warm, secure, already sensing that he is loved. And
now he drifts off into his first sleep.

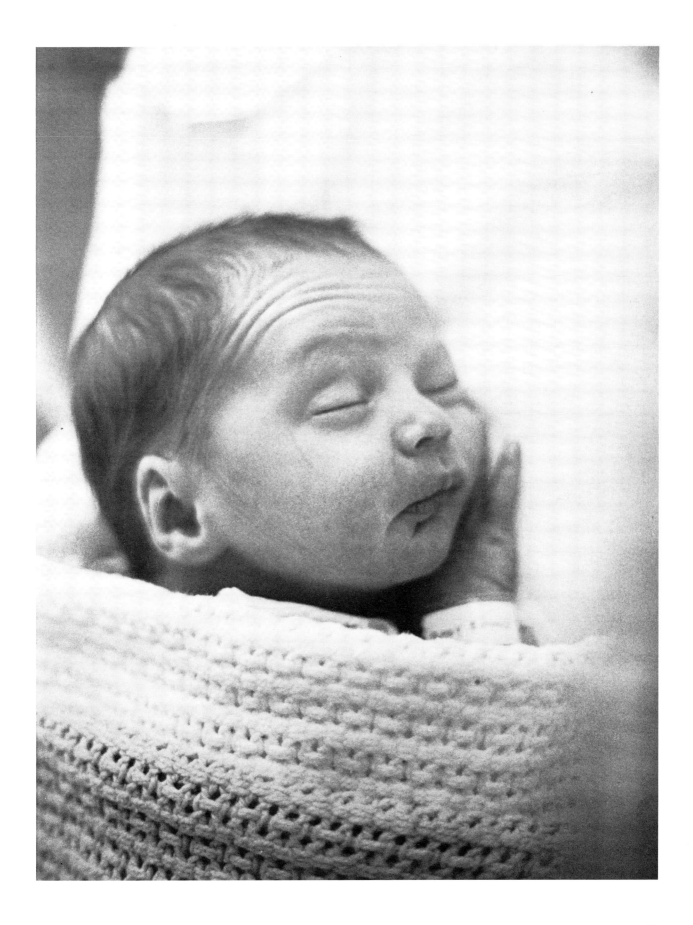

The First Week

Newborn babies seem totally helpless and floppy. But they have several extraordinary abilities.

Though they will not learn to walk by themselves probably for a year or more, yet, immediately, they have a walk *reflex*. When their feet touch the ground, they cannot help making walking movements.

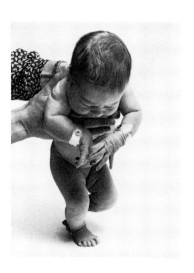

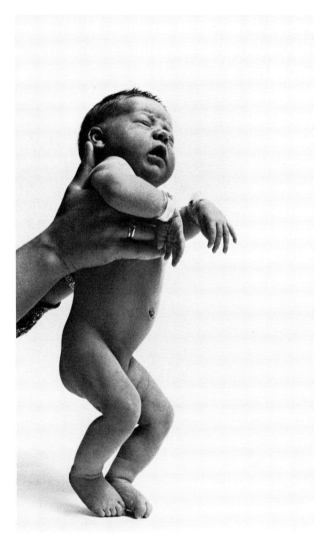

The doctor tests baby Liza. . . for a moment she seems to crumple, then . . .

. . . suddenly she seems to feel her weight . . .

40

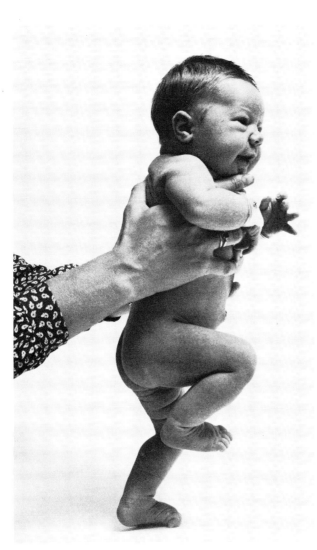

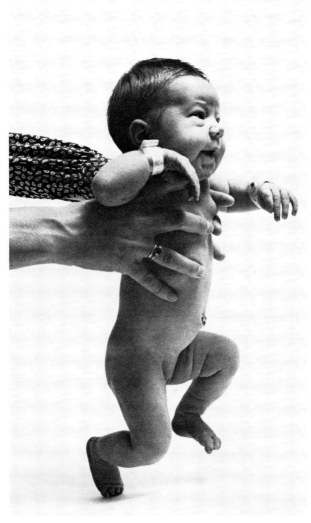

... right foot forward ...

...left foot forward. Quick march! This walk reflex disappears after ten days or two weeks.

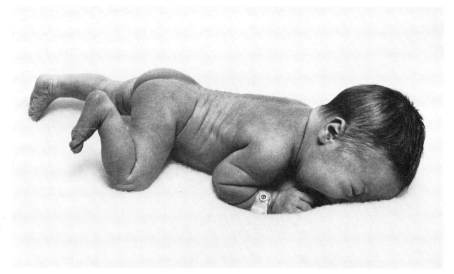

Babies also have a crawl reflex. Though they cannot move along, their legs make energetic crawling movements . . .

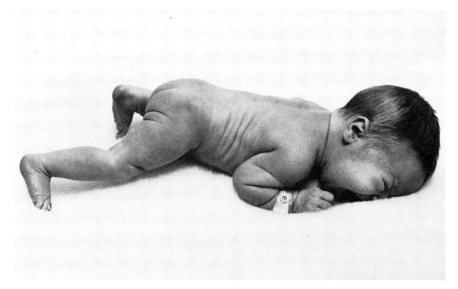

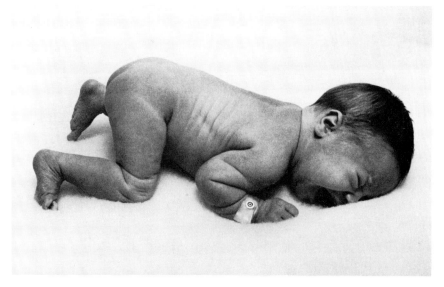

. . . and if they are placed on their stomachs, they know by instinct that they must move their heads so that they cannot suffocate.

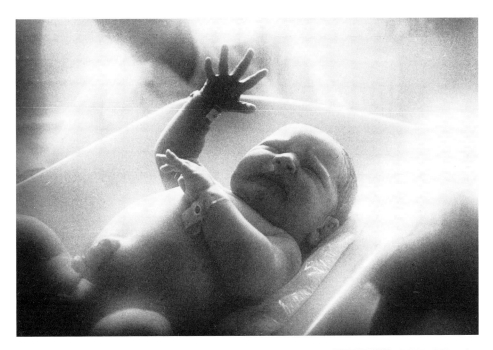

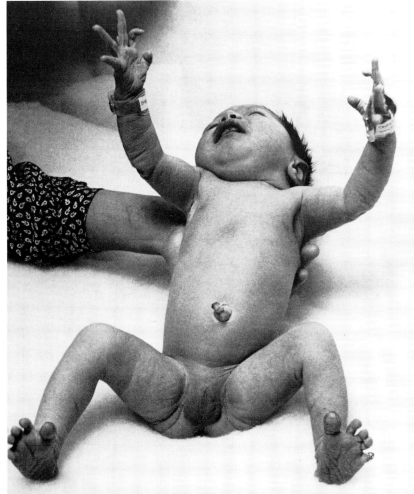

Babies are happier when they are wrapped up firmly in a blanket. They feel insecure if their arms are left free and they are not totally supported.

Though too young ever to have experienced danger, they seem to throw out their arms to save themselves, often spreading their fingers wide. They are not actually afraid of falling: this is a reflex action triggered off instinctively when they feel unsafe.

The grip reflex is shared by baby humans and animals.

A kitten can hold on for herself . . .

A baby monkey has to be able to grip his mother while she leaps from tree to tree. . .

Babies can hold on too. A human baby can be lifted up, right off the ground by the strength of his own grip (though children must not try testing this on their new brothers or sisters as occasionally a baby can let go!).

But it's safe – and interesting – to test the strength of the baby's grip, for anyone who is not afraid of a good, hard pinch. The grip is so strong that the blood runs from the baby's finger-tips, and they sometimes go quite white.

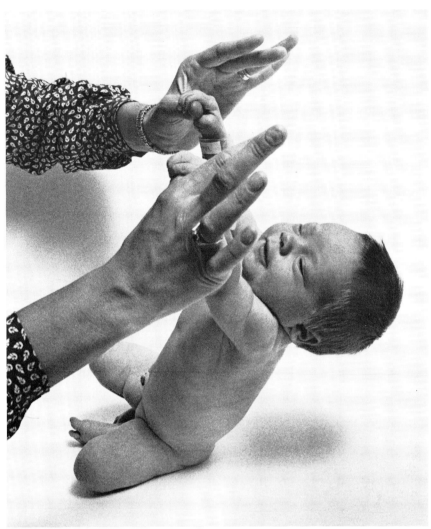

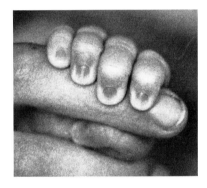

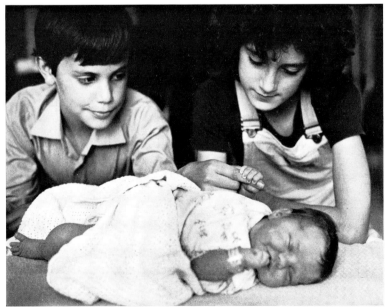

His toes grip too, just like those of a little monkey.

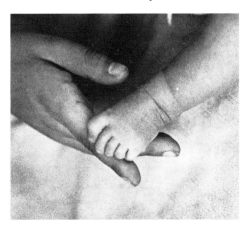

The reflex to suck was present in the baby even before his birth.

For the first few days after birth, instead of ordinary breast milk, the mother produces a special, easily digestible liquid called *colostrum*.

Colostrum contains extra protein and is the perfect nourishment for the baby's delicate stomach. It also carries from the mother to the baby a resistance to the germs he or she will meet in the outside world.

So by breast-feeding, the mother is giving her baby more than mere food. She is giving him protection from illness too.

The bottle-fed baby misses out on this protection.

But hopefully he will get just as much cuddling and love. A baby that is not cuddled does not thrive as well as one which receives a full diet of love and attention. Babies need to feel loved as much as they need food.

A first-time mother can mostly rely on 'mother's instinct'. But she may need help to learn to understand the exact needs of her individual baby over food, and to recognise why he is crying; perhaps he is still hungry after his feed, or perhaps he still wants the comfort of suckling even though he has had enough milk.

She has to practise the right way to swaddle the baby to make him feel secure; and know how to change him and care for him and clean him, sometimes a very messy job. She also has to learn how to support her baby safely in the bath. Usually a specially trained nursery-nurse gives the new mother some help.

First attempts with a slippery, wet, wriggly baby can be quite unnerving. Many babies hate baths. But if a baby happens to like water, bath time is one of the most enjoyable moments of the day.

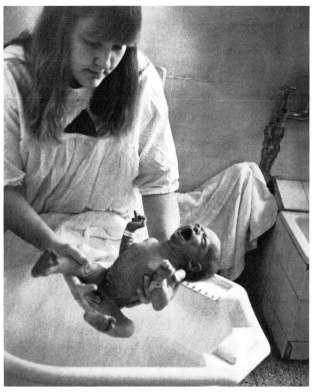

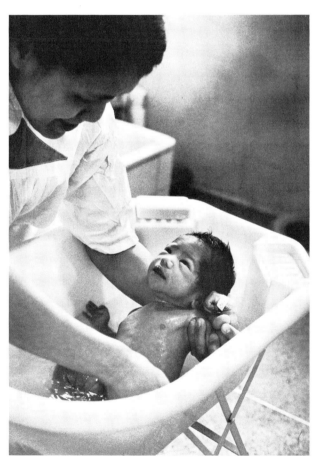

So not only is the new mother resting after her labour and the birth, but during her week or so in hospital she has an opportunity to practise caring for her baby with friendly nurses close by to help. Brothers and sisters also have a chance to see a little of the new member of their family before he comes home.

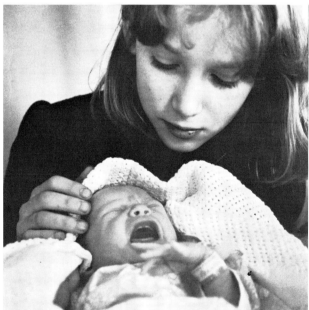

Babies in Special Care

Most babies have their cots in the hospital wards, next to their mothers' beds, at least during the day.

However, a few babies are delicate and have to be looked after in the Special Care Unit. Usually this happens because a baby has been born one or two months before the due date.

Baby Bobby was born exceptionally early, after just 26 weeks instead of 38 inside his mother's womb. He weighed only one kilo (the average new baby weighs about 3½ kilos). He looked perfect but his tiny lungs were not yet strong enough to breathe for him, and his own heat-generating mechanism was not developed enough for him to keep warm just with blankets and clothes.

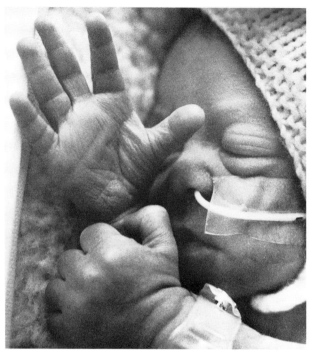

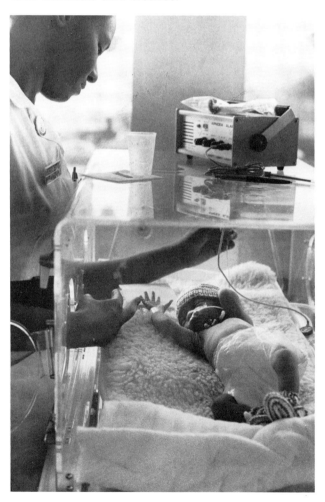

So for several weeks he had to live in an *incubator.* Inside the plastic covering, the temperature was much the same as inside the mother's womb. His devoted nurses knitted him miniature boots and caps to keep the top of his head and his toes extra warm. And under the soft sheepskin mat, an electronic sensor was monitoring his breathing: any change in rhythm, and the alarm would ring, then a nurse would come quickly to make sure he was all right.

Until his lungs were stronger, a *ventilating machine* pumped the air in and out, breathing for him. Even after his lungs had started to pump the air properly, he still needed extra oxygen for several more weeks to keep him alive.

Baby Bobby was not strong enough to suck for some weeks, so his milk had to be fed through a thin, soft tube. In his mouth the tube would have got in the way of his tongue, and it was much more comfortable for him to have it running through his nostril down into his throat. The milk came from his mother though he wasn't strong enough to suck from her. She went every day to the hospital to give her milk and to stroke and to talk to Bobby.

As soon as Bobby was strong enough to breathe for a short while without extra oxygen, he was allowed out of his incubator for a cuddle with his mother. Even the most delicate babies, struggling for life, need to sense human love and care in order to thrive.

About two months after he was born – almost at the exact time he was actually due – Bobby gave his mother his first smile. . .

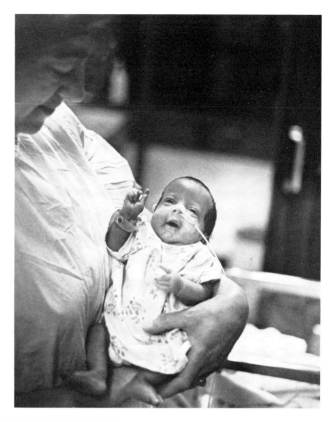

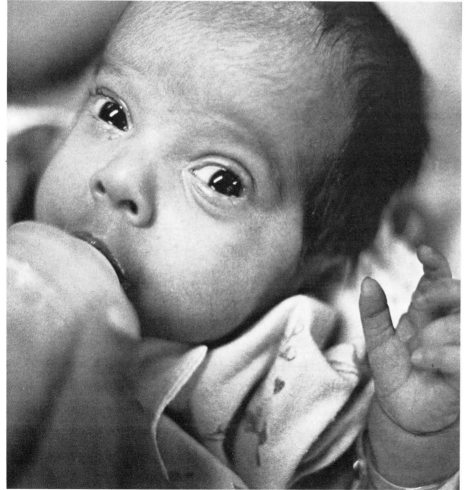

About that time he began to suck some of his milk from a bottle, and soon he was strong enough to manage to suck all the milk he needed, so his tube could be removed.

After three months, his mother was able to take him home to join his brothers and sister. He was still slightly delicate, but within a few months he had caught up with other babies the same age and was round and plump and healthy.

The nursing of *premature babies* like Bobby is a demanding but interesting job. Someone is on watch night and day, and it is only through the nurses' devoted care that a baby like Bobby can survive.

In most, but not all hospitals, Special Care Units expect their visitors to dress up in sterilised, ultra-clean, hospital overalls, to avoid bringing infection to the babies. Nowadays brothers and sisters are usually allowed to visit because it is important for the baby to become part of the family even if he or she has to spend most of the time in an incubator.

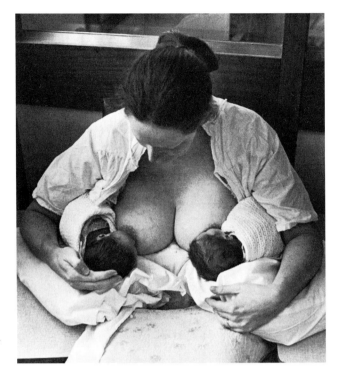

Not all babies are born early, like Bobby. Usually *twins* are smaller than single babies, and may have to spend a while in the Special Care Unit. These tiny, delicate twins will need constant attention and frequent feeds for many weeks after they come out of hospital. Their mother is lucky to have a willing ten-year-old daughter to help.

If the babies are large and strong enough to suck for themselves, naturally they are best off being breast fed.

When premature babies are too small and weak to suck, so that their milk has to be fed to them through tubes, the mothers can still provide their own milk for the babies, using a breast pump. Breast milk is obviously much better for babies than the powdered milk from cows, which is sold commercially for babies' bottles.

It is usually just an accident of nature and not the mother's fault that a baby is born early or delicate enough to need Special Care. However, sometimes if a woman smokes too much during pregnancy, she will have an undersized baby. And some women cause even more tragic harm to the fetus inside them.

Sue is the daughter of a drug addict.

Her mother was taking drugs all through pregnancy. And because everything that a mother eats, smokes or drinks gets processed through the cord into the baby's digestive system, Sue, long before she was born, was absorbing some of her mother's daily 'fix' of drugs.

So poor little Sue was born a drug addict! She screamed night and day for drugs. She kicked and struggled hour after hour in her incubator, suffering the real agony of withdrawal symptoms – like older drug addicts who cannot get at their supplies. She could not keep her food down. She was in danger of having fits which might leave her mentally handicapped for the rest of her life. All because her mother could not give up drugs even when she was pregnant.

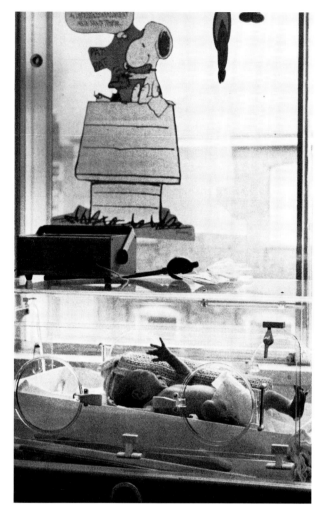

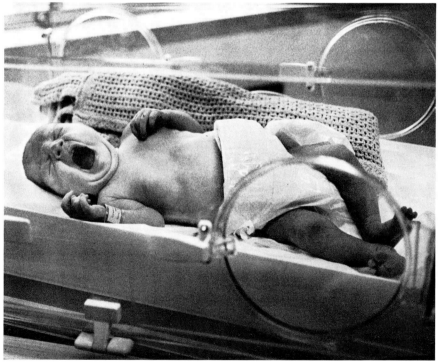

Fortunately the doctors and nurses were able to save Sue. To wean her off her addiction, they had to give her small doses of the drug, reducing the amount every day, until at last Sue could manage without any.

Now she is in a foster home, waiting for the moment when her mother can be cured of the drug habit, and become a responsible enough person to care for her own baby.

Special Care babies are in hospital sometimes for weeks, sometimes for only a few days.

Ordinary babies also stay for a varying amount of time. Mothers with first babies are usually given longer to get used to feeding and bathing and caring for their babies. More experienced mothers sometimes go home within a few hours of the baby's birth, so that they can be with their other chidren who may be missing them.

Bringing the baby home for the first time is always an exciting moment.

Help from Older Children

Once home the mother needs all the help she can get, from her husband, her older children, neighbours or friends. Though the hospital will have passed her as fit to come home, it will be several weeks before she is back to full strength.

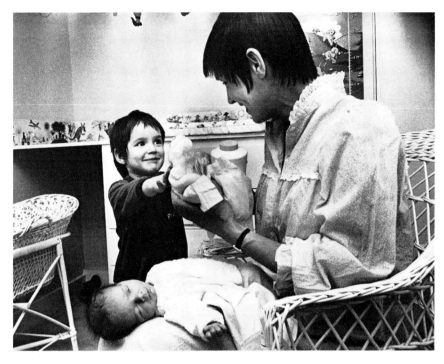

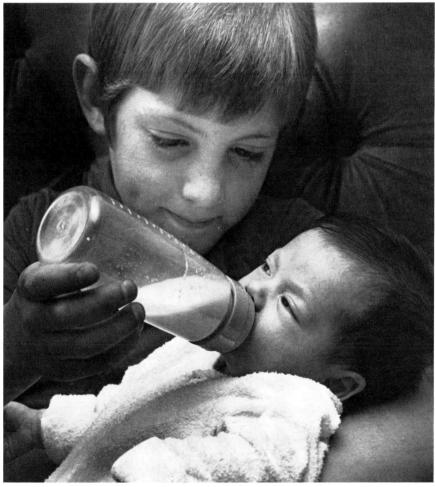

Even the youngest child can help, bringing something her mother has forgotten. . .

. . . an older child may give an occasional bottle of boiled water if the baby is breast fed .

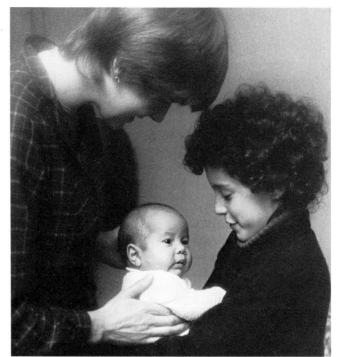

Parents of new babies can become exhausted if the baby is keeping them up at night. So an elder brother or sister sometimes needs to be understanding and comforting to a tired, or even irritable mother. Taking the baby off the mother's hands for a while can make all the difference to a mother who seems to do little else but look after the baby.

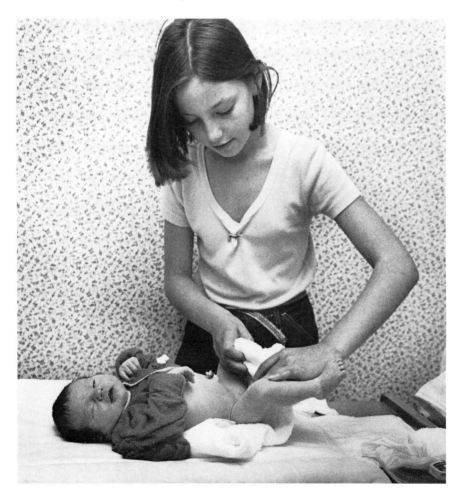

Even the tiniest baby loves to have someone talking to him. He will stare up fascinated. And he will learn to talk long before the baby who is rocked silently.

A baby who never hears speech can never absorb it naturally. It is not just a question of the baby's intelligence – or the mother's. The cleverest women are sometimes the least help to their babies, like a certain university professor. An extremely learned woman, she could make complicated statements to other adults, but felt foolish talking to her baby. So he did not pick up even the simplest words: he still could not speak when he was four.

The best parents – and brothers and sisters – talk gently to the baby: 'Now I'm going to wash your face. Now dry it. Now tuck you into your cot.' And babies love to be sung to, any simple little song.

Some couples, until they have their own babies, cannot help treating their pets as if they were their children.

Cats and dogs can become deeply jealous of a new baby who seems to be taking their place. So another valuable way a young friend or neighbour can help a new mother is to take the dog for a walk or play with the cat, especially at the baby's feeding time. . .

The arrival of a new baby can be shattering for a toddler too. For his whole short life he may have been his mother's only adored child. Then she suddenly disappears into hospital and comes back with a new baby, who takes so much of her attention.

When a toddler is too young to understand, he can turn – in a few days – from a happy, contented child into a jealous, very angry small person. It can take him years to get over his jealousy. Some children go on quarrelling and feeling jealous of a brother or sister even after they've grown up

If a responsible older child can play with the toddler, keeping him busy, making him feel loved and cared for while the mother carries on with the necessary work of feeding and caring for the baby, the jealousy won't hurt the toddler so much, and he will get on better with his new brother or sister all through childhood.

A clever mother (or brother or sister) will have taken care to prepare the toddler for the arrival of the new baby. Rosina had to prepare her two-year-old daughter, Rosie, for the arrival of twins – so she bought twin dolls, and played games with Rosie, bathing them and putting them to bed.

Rosie was thrilled when her mother brought the real twins home.

The only trouble was that Rosie really shouldn't have tried to test whether the real twins' eyes opened and shut like the dolls'. . .

Growing Up

A human baby develops much slower than other mammals, many of which can walk almost as soon as they are born.

At birth the human baby is so floppy he cannot hold up the weight of his own head . . .

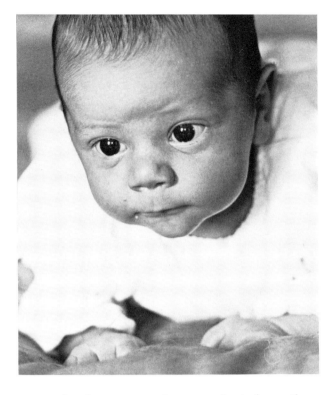

. . . it takes him two or three weeks to have the strength to lift his head for a few seconds to look around him. . .

It takes several months to be strong enough to roll over, and five or six months before he can sit up by himself. . .

Going . . .   going . . .   gone!

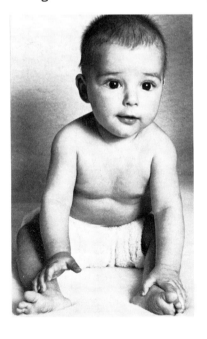

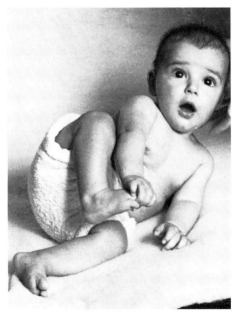

The next stage is crawling. Sometimes though he tries to crawl forwards, he only succeeds in going backwards, away from the object of his desire, which he finds very puzzling.

Thereafter he may be of the opinion that he can feed himself perfectly well without help. . .

The great moment will arrive when he takes his first wobbly, staggering steps. . .
Soon he will be talking, running, jumping. . .

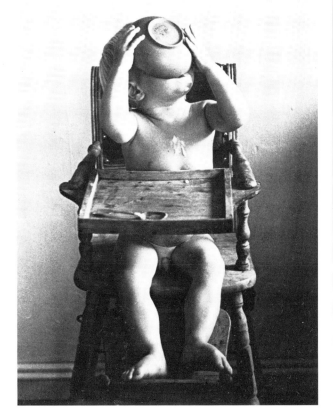 

And so the babies become toddlers, the toddlers become schoolchildren, and the schoolchildren start to grow up. Then they will fall in love, get married, and the whole story will start over again. . .

Glossary

Amniotic fluid Liquid in which the unborn baby floats in his mother's womb.

Breech birth The baby is born bottom (or feet) first, instead of the normal head-first presentation.

Birth canal The vagina in a softened and flexible condition at the end of the pregnancy. (See page 22.)

Caesarian section Due to some medical complication, some babies are born by surgery rather than by normal labour.

The surgeon operates and lifts the baby out of a cut in the mother's abdomen. The mother is then stitched up, as after an appendix operation, and is left with a scar. The baby is not usually much affected: in fact from his point of view, this may be the quickest and easiest way out. This operation is named after Julius Caesar who was said to be born this way.

Cells A complex blob of jelly, the smallest unit of the human body, which is made up of billions of cells.

Colostrum Extremely valuable liquid, not exactly milk, the baby receives from his mother in the first few days after birth. Colostrum is of high protein content with elements which protect the newborn baby from infection.

Conception The moment when a woman's ripe egg is fertilised by a man's sperm, and the baby begins to grow. The egg and sperm join together to make one cell, which divides again and again and grows into a baby.

Contraction During labour the mother's muscles contract, pulling open the entrance to her womb, in order to form the birth canal through which the baby can leave her body. Towards the end of her labour, the muscular contractions change their function, and help her to push her baby down the birth canal and out into the world.

Egg (*Ovum*) The eggs develop in the ovaries at each end of the fallopian tubes. One egg ripens every month, first from one ovary (egg store), then the other, and works its way along the tube. If at this stage it is fertilised by sperm from a man, it continues and burrows into the wall of the womb, and grows into an embryo. If it is not fertilised, it comes out unnoticed before the woman's monthly period. (See Maturity.)

Embryo The developing baby in its earliest stages, during the first twelve weeks after the mother's egg has been fertilised by the man's sperm. (See page 10.)

Fetus After twelve weeks, the EMBRYO has developed to the point of really looking like a human baby, and, from this stage until birth, is called a FETUS. (See page 11.)

Forceps Doctor's instruments to help gently draw the baby out of the mother if she needs some extra help.

Incubator A heated, closed-in bed, a mechanical substitute for the mother's womb, mostly used for babies who have been born early and could not survive without extra warmth and extra oxygen. Incubators are also used to sustain the life of sick babies. Inside the incubator, an electronically-sensitised mattress will set off an alarm if the baby stops breathing even for a moment, so that a nurse can rush to the rescue, and save the baby's life.

Labour Labour is the time just before birth when first the womb muscles open the way out so that the baby can come down through the birth canal and out of the mother.

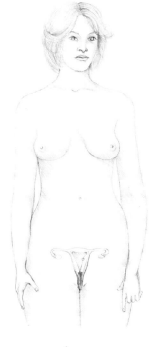

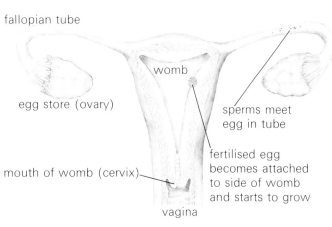

fallopian tube

womb

egg store (ovary)

sperms meet egg in tube

fertilised egg becomes attached to side of womb and starts to grow

mouth of womb (cervix)

vagina

Maturity (Puberty) – Girls A girl reaches maturity, otherwise known as puberty, when she has her first monthly period. Most girls have their first periods roughly between the ages of ten and fifteen. Once the periods start, she would be capable of having a baby, if one of her eggs were to be fertilised by a man. From the time she starts her regular periods, each month her womb will grow a new lining, like a bed for the baby to settle into.

Once this lining is ready, if a ripe egg has been fertilised by a man's sperm, it will settle into the lining and start to grow. If the egg is not fertilised, the lining is shed each month in the form of a thin red stream of blood and debris. This is called a period. It lasts for a few days of every month for every mature girl and woman except when she is pregnant, or too old to have babies. Once the flow is finished, the womb then grows a new lining in case the next egg is transformed into an embryo by a sperm. This way, the woman's womb is always fresh and ready to support a new life.

Maturity (Puberty) – Boys Boys mature on average at a slightly older age than girls, somewhere around fourteen to sixteen. They are capable of fatherhood once their testicles have started to produce sperms.

In other countries and other civilisations, also in past European history, young people have been allowed to marry and have children earlier than in our society. However this was usually when all generations of the family lived close together, and the young couples probably remained for some years under their parents' roofs. Nowadays we live in a more complex and difficult world, and young people are advised to wait until they are grown up, established in life and able to earn their livings before they take on the joys and the great responsibilities of parenthood.

Midwife Man or woman specially trained in the care of expectant mothers, delivering babies and looking after the mother and baby immediately after birth. Most midwives have trained as nurses before starting on midwifery.

Navel (*Umbilicus*) Otherwise known as the belly-button. The scar left when the umbilical cord has shrivelled away and dropped off.

Painkillers (*Drugs*) Chemicals which can help some mothers who feel pain or discomfort during the contraction of the womb; also used if the doctors have to use forceps to help the baby to be born.

Penis The organ of the male body used both for urinating and for passing sperm into the female to create babies. The penis is just a channel. The urine comes from the bladder along one passage. The sperms, produced in the testicles and stored until needed in the epididymis (see diagram), travel when the man makes love to the woman, along a completely different passage, which eventually joins into the same tube used by the

urine. However, the urine passage is completely shut off during lovemaking so that there is no possibility of urine passing from the man into the woman's vagina.

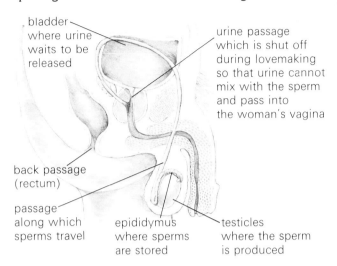

bladder where urine waits to be released

urine passage which is shut off during lovemaking so that urine cannot mix with the sperm and pass into the woman's vagina

back passage (rectum)

passage along which sperms travel

epididymus where sperms are stored

testicles where the sperm is produced

Placenta A special organ which forms in the womb while the baby develops. It takes food and oxygen from the mother and returns the baby's waste products.

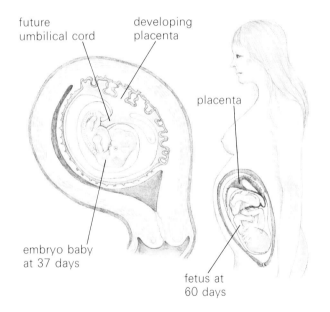

future umbilical cord

developing placenta

placenta

embryo baby at 37 days

fetus at 60 days

Premature babies Babies born before their full 38 weeks inside their mothers. A baby born after about 25 weeks in the womb is about the youngest that can survive, but he is seriously at risk. Babies born after 30 or 31 weeks are easier to cope with and those born at 33 or 34 weeks may be able to come out of the incubator comparatively quickly. Before the invention of incubators, many premature babies died. Several famous people were born prematurely, including Winston Churchill.

Reflexes An involuntary action which a baby cannot help making, such as the walking reflex (*see* pages 40/41). The baby automatically finds himself lifting his feet when they touch a solid surface.

Sperm Minute seed of a man, which, joined with a woman's egg will start growing into an embryo. The sperm has a tiny round head and a thin tail which helps it to swim up through the woman's womb and up into the egg tube. Only the most vigorous sperm succeed in reaching an egg. The man's testicles manufacture billions of sperm during his lifetime; every time a man makes love to a woman he passes into her about two million sperm, though only one can fertilise one egg. Nature seems very determined that the human species shall not die out. (The same goes for animals and plants.)

out of millions of sperm, only one succeeds in joining the egg

Twins Identical twins, who look *exactly* alike and are either both boys or both girls, always develop from one egg fertilsed by one sperm. The egg then divides into twins rather than developing as a single baby. The identical twins each have their own umbilical cord, but obtain their nourishment and their oxygen from one shared placenta.

Unidentical twins (sometimes called fraternal twins) are conceived if the mother has two eggs passing through her fallopian tubes rather than the usual egg per month. These two eggs are then fertilised by two sperms and then settle independently into the lining of the mother's womb. Each unidentical twin has its own placenta. They may be both the same sex or one of each.

Twins commonly occur where there is a family history, say a grandparent who was a twin, or twin great-aunts, or cousins.

Identical twins   Unidentical twins

placenta   placenta

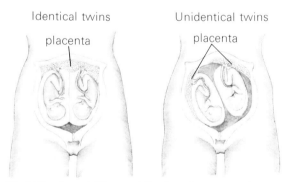

Umbilical cord The umbilical cord consists of two intertwined arteries and one vein encased in a jelly-like skin. It carries all food, blood and oxygen to the unborn baby and carries away all waste materials.

Vagina Passageway to and from the woman's womb. A soft, flexible area, it becomes even more stretchy when a woman is expecting a baby. It is made in folds which open out during birth.

The vagina is totally separate from the passage which carries urine out from the bladder. (The urine emerges from a small, star-shaped hole in front of the much larger opening of the vagina.)

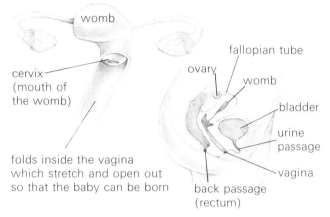

womb

fallopian tube

cervix (mouth of the womb)

ovary

womb

bladder

urine passage

folds inside the vagina which stretch and open out so that the baby can be born

vagina

back passage (rectum)

Ventilator If a baby is born more than six weeks early, his lungs may not be sufficiently well formed to inflate and fill with oxygen, then deflate to expel carbon dioxide. A ventilating machine gently inflates and deflates the premature baby's lungs so that he can breathe.

Vernix The whole time that the baby is in the womb, he is floating in amniotic fluid. Until the last few weeks before he is born, he is covered in a protective white grease, so that his skin will not become dried and wrinkled like a washer-woman's fingers by constant immersion in liquid. If a baby is born early, he may still be covered in vernix (*see* page 29). If he is born late, and the vernix has worn off some time before, he may have very dry wrinkled skin and long finger nails.

Womb (*Uterus*) A small hollow bag of muscle, the size and shape of a pear, inside every female. Once the fertilised egg becomes attached to the lining of the womb and starts to grow into an embryo, the womb gradually expands to exactly the right size to contain the baby floating safely in the amniotic fluid.

amniotic fluid

"wall" of womb

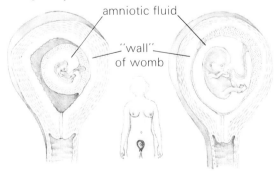